Zen Ventures

The Future of Venture Capital & Impact Investing

By

Champion Muthle

Copyright © 2021 Champion Muthle

All rights reserved.

ISBN: 9798501102460

DEDICATION

To the homeless kids in the rain.
I haven't forgotten you.

CONTENTS

	Acknowledgments	i
1	Zen Ventures	1
2	The Venture Vortex	5
3	The New Path	11
4	Finding & Staying Zen	18
5	The Six Myths (1 & 2)	23
6	The Six Myths (3 & 4)	32
7	The Six Myths (5 & 6)	42
8	Our Vision & Model	49
9	Our Startups & Portfolio	57
10	The Future of Venture Capital & Impact Investing	83

ACKNOWLEDGMENTS

A special thanks to all my investors and supporters throughout the years. Our value and impact continues to increase. More to come.

1

ZEN VENTURES

Control your own destiny or someone else will.

- Jack Welch

It should come as no surprise, especially to diverse founders, that the flow of investment capital is controlled by a small group of predominantly White male elites. This we already know. What's disturbing is that these investments are made to look like rational, objective and unbiased decisions. In reality, we know this isn't true. In fact, we've known for quite a long time now that these investments favor a select group of predominantly White male founders, and reinforce some of the worst socioeconomic inequalities in the World. Instead of Silicon Valley it should be called "The Great Money Heist." Instead of Venture Capital, it should be called "Generational Wealth Transfer," because that's exactly what it amounts to. Let's face it, VCs are in the business of selling money, not investing in good ideas and incredible Founders. When life ends, Venture Capitalists will still be asking Founders and Startups for more proof points.

Yet thanks to these very same forces, this system doesn't seem to be changing anytime soon. Meanwhile, back on Wall Street, a predominantly White group of Private Equity Barons quietly controls the allocation of Credit and Capital in a manner that we've already seen destroy the economy. The longer this broken and corrupt system continues, the worse off our countries will be, and the higher the burden of debt the next generation will inherit. In this business, access is structured like a Hollywood pyramid scheme: Pay to play. The more you buy into the hype, the higher up you get in the scheme.

All around the world, however, there are groups of entrepreneurs and innovators who are beginning to change things; they're taking a good, critical look at the current state of play, and marshalling every resource at their disposal to shift us in a new direction, and into a better world. This group realizes that, for most part, the flow of capital is based on an outdated set of stereotypes and myths that are reinforced and perpetuated by the system itself. The solutions this group brings to the table over the next few years, and the partnerships they form in the pursuit of equity, inclusion, and equality will define the future of Venture Capital, and the global economy, for decades to come.

What's needed is a revolution in Venture Capital: A shift in mindset, and a more mature approach to the Market that takes into account pre-existing economic and social inequities, biases and imbalances. This new mindset, methodology, and movement within Venture Capital starts with an openness to Diversity in all its forms, true Evolution, and a New Economics. An Economics that expands the room and gives birth to lifestyles based on ethical investing, goodwill, and good business above all else. Enter Zen Ventures. This is where our journey begins.

2

THE VENTURE VORTEX

The temptation to give up is strongest just before victory.

- Zen Proverb

I had to go through hell to get to heaven. When I landed in hell, I put out a chair and put up a sign: "Free Consultations - Startups, Business Plans, Resumes." After a few minutes, my first customer arrived. A bright young guy looking to start an eco-friendly recycling business. Although I didn't know it at the time, that was the start of my venture studio. Later on, while walking the beaches of Hawaii, I landed on a name for the new endeavor, Zen Ventures, an impact venture studio for diverse founders.

The breakthrough came in the aftermath of a real debacle. A year earlier I had traveled to Menorca, Spain (the small Island) to attend an incubator for my newest startup, AdHeat, an exciting new AdTech platform. AdHeat had been selected out of over thousands of startups from around the world and was the best looking business in the entire group. An idyllic sea-side incubator in the middle of the Mediterranean, how could I say no?

Two weeks later, disaster. What was supposed to be an empty Island with supportive investors was packed with nosey tourists and noisy little kids. The staff were friendly enough, but someone seemed intent on sabotaging the whole thing. That's when something truly strange happened, something I still struggle to understand to this day. The incubator turned on me. There was a clear intent to block my progress, but I couldn't figure out why. Sure I was the only black guy, but there was something far more sinister happening than just racism. Let's just say it didn't go well, but not for lack of trying. I arrived with my startup intact and left with it broken…at an incubator. In hindsight, it was a clear scam. I suppose the Pirate flag atop the grand water park should have been a dead giveaway.

Unfortunately, as I later discovered, this is a common occurrence in the highly competitive world of Venture Capital. Jim McKelvey, the Cofounder of Square, talks about this in his inspiring and entertaining book, *The*

Innovation Stack (Portfolio, 2020). On top of all this, I returned home to find that the investors I had been speaking to in the United States had pulled out, stolen my idea, and illegally created a mirror image copy of my platform, down to the density map, my proprietary technique. I was furious. This was supposed to be my first exit, but instead it ended up being my demise. My entire world was turned upside down in the blink of an eye.

I had encountered this kind of corruption before as a young man growing up in South Africa. My father was in politics. I also witnessed it in the United States as a young Civil Rights Leader. It disgusted me then just as much as it disgusted me now. Despite taking every precaution, every consideration, and having nothing but the best of intentions, I had become the victim of con artists and corporate criminals yet again. As President George Bush famously said, "Fool me once, shame on you. Fool me twice, shame on me. Fool me a third time…well, you're not gonna fool me again!"

I was now broke, unemployed and without a startup despite having saved my money wisely, spent my money perfectly, and planned my life diligently. My girlfriend and I had broken up prior to my heading to Spain, so now it was just me. My friends were all in Prague where I had lived for a short time before moving back to LA. There I was, all alone in Los Angeles without a penny in my pocket. I tried to take the culprits to court, but encountered an equally corrupt set of judges and attorneys. Really. My only choice was to move on, move forward, and rebuild. So that's what I did, for the second or third time in my adult life.

Despite being a Civil Rights Leader, despite being on the Forbes List, and despite being an Award-winning Strategist, my second company was now a flop. I couldn't help but feel like everybody and their mother was laughing at me, and not for the first time.

Later on, I came to find out that, in the age of fake news, someone had run what can only be described as a deepfake and adversarial attack against me. But none of that mattered now, the damage had already been done. I tried to report this to the FBI several times, but was laughed out of the building. By law, they're required to provide people with progress reports once a case has been filed. Four years later, I've still yet to hear back from them. Not even so much as a phone call or email. The message was clear, either give up or move on. This was the cold reality of the world I was thrown into at the height of my entrepreneurial endeavors. This was the cold reality of Venture Capital. This was the Venture Vortex.

3

THE NEW PATH

A thousand-mile journey begins with just one step.

- Zen Proverb

After the "Red Wedding" that was my first foray into Venture Capital, I needed time to reset, recuperate, and recover from my extensive wounds. I needed time to figure out what had just happened, and consider if this was still a path I wanted to pursue. I had to start over and rethink the industry completely. I had to forget everything I knew or thought I knew about, well, almost everything, including Venture Capital. I had to dredge the depths of my soul, and the industry itself, to figure out what exactly had gone wrong, why, and how to fix it. This would mean reassessing the entire philosophical and economic framework of venture capital and adjusting for false imperatives, cognitive biases, untruths, and flat out lies. It meant investigating the very foundation of venture capital and private equity, uncovering their very structure and system of belief (or rather, their cult of personality), and adjusting for inflation and slippage.

I thought that if I learned everything there was to learn about the industry there was no way I couldn't be successful. Boy was I wrong. In reality, there was a secret room I wasn't being let into, a hidden hand maneuvering against me, a glass ceiling hovering right above me the whole time. And as I would come to find out, in this industry, there really are no rules, no limit to what people are capable of, especially if you're a diverse founder.

Fortunately, the one thing I didn't have to relearn was Entrepreneurship, that I already had down pat. After several entrepreneurial successes as a youngster and throughout high school and college, I was proud to be inducted into the Forbes List for Social Entrepreneurship at the age of 26. I sat on the list next to Malala Yousafzai and 28 of the other most impactful social entrepreneurs in the world. It was the first year Social Entrepreneurship and Social Impact were included on the list. I was very proud to be a member of that inaugural class of changemakers. And we were ready to change the world yet again.

Having to forget and reformulate everything I knew, or thought I knew about the industry wasn't easy; but in so doing, I stumbled upon a new, more meaningful, meditative, and fulfilling way of life and business that would become the very foundation of Zen Ventures.

As the son of an Olympic Runner, everyday I try to work out, meditate and go running or do Martial Arts. I focus on positivity, meaningful action, and intentionality. I try to be mindful of my energy, the environment, and the people around me. I try to eat healthy, reduce, toxins and limit bad habits. It's not just about being healthy and fit, it's about having focus, drive, and sustainable energy. It's about work-life balance and the ease of doing business. People will tell you "No" a million times in this industry, usually for stupid reasons. You can't let it get to you. You've gotta stay focused, not put any roadblocks in your way, and not let any negative people block your path. It's about protecting and empowering your particular truth, spirit, and passions as much as possible. And, in a world so desperate for money, fame, and power, it's about remembering what really matters to you, rather than what everyone else wants to see or what everyone else thinks matters. Just like in the movie *The Big Short*. The same lessons from the film apply to Venture Capital. Don't let the system short you, don't fall victim to misinformation, and for the love of God, think for yourself.

Forget what people think about the size of your Series A or the readiness of your MVP. It's not all about speed and flashy Term Sheets. It's about developing products you love and putting things on the market that you can stand by. Because no matter what, there's bound to be a few harsh critics, jaded investors, and unhappy customers out there. As we've seen in films like *The Social Network*, Silicon Valley is basically a glorified popularity contest, boys club and beauty pageant. It's driven by an assortment of biases, stereotypes, and bad logic. The goal is to create chaos and uncertainty so that money can swoop in, take over, and feast off the value that you created.

Ironically, the new lifestyle I came to adopt after the ridiculousness of infringing investors and corporate pirates was similar to the one I had lived as a child. As a boy, I was incredibly passionate about Martial Arts. By the time I was 17, I had done 7 years of Kenpo, 3 years of Shotokan, 3 years of Aikido, 2 years of Yoga, and 1 year of Budokan. As a competitive Athlete and World Championship Qualifier, I was no stranger to hard work and discipline. My father was often criticized for being one of the hardest working athletes in Track & Field. And my mother was a Collegiate Sprinter. I grew up running Track & Field, playing Soccer, Football, Volleyball, and the Drums. The amount of discipline and drive it took to do all this while maintaining a 3.85 GPA was good preparation for Venture Capital.

As a founder there are lots of moving pieces and difficult personalities to deal with, not to mention the constraints of being Black and underfunded. Being able to swim gracefully in these waters is a critical skill. One must become a master juggler, diplomat, and fundraiser, or risk having no fun at all. And if you're not having fun, you're not doing it right. Creativity, playfulness, and a sense of humor are essential elements of the Entrepreneur's playbook. As I wrote in 2014 after making the Forbes List, the Top Five Traits of Social Entrepreneurs are: Compassion, Curiosity, Courage, Creativity, and Conviction. There was just one element I was missing all those years ago, which I finally found in Hawaii: Zen.

4

FINDING & STAYING ZEN

To be for one day entirely at leisure is to be for one day an immortal.

- Chinese Proverb

I was admittedly a late bloomer to Buddhism. I discovered its deeper purpose and power after dating a Russian Kalmyk girl while living in Prague. Like most Russian women, she was beautiful and brilliant. Although you wouldn't think it given its focus on non-violence, Buddhism is one of the most powerful practices in the world. You would do well not to mess with a Buddhist. Underneath those Monkish orange robes is a mind of steel and a heart of pure gold. Not to mention an energy and psychic power to match that of Royalty and the Rosicrucians. Something I learned the hard way after showing up a bit late for dinner one night.

The Noble Eightfold Path, the Wheel of Time, and the Tibetan Book of the Dead are just a few excellent guides and ways of thinking that Buddhism brings to Commerce and Venture Capital. The Eightfold Path can be seen as the path walked by the Entrepreneur, and The Book of the Dead itself can be viewed as a metaphor for the evolution of startups and founders themselves—a painful cycle of rebirth (*pivots*), leading to liberation from world (*samsara*) in the form Nirvana

(Term Sheets, an Exit, or an IPO).

Central to the Buddhist Religion and Philosophy are the ideas of ethical enquiry, compassion, and *Rightfulness*: Right View, Right Intention, Right Speech, Right Action, Right Livelihood, Right Effort, Right Mindfulness, and Right Concentration. The Path itself reflects the startup ideation process: Moral Virtue (Problem/Solution), Meditation (Idea/Hypothesis), and Insight or Wisdom (Insight/Execution). Like the African Philosophy of Ubuntu, Buddhist views of society and culture are also reflected in the Entrepreneurial spirit of Community and Foundry—safe havens where founders and startups can grow and thrive together. It's all about understanding cause and effect. I am because we are. We exist in oneness with each other. What brings me down brings you down, too. What lifts me up, lifts you up, too.

Good health, meditation, and positivity are just the beginning. The principles of Zen Buddhism can be applied to the entire startup and Venture Capital process, from designing the idea and solution to building the MVP and negotiating the Term Sheet, Exit, Acquisition or IPO. As a Social Entrepreneur, community and environmental considerations are inextricably linked to the big idea and process itself. Passion, purpose, and ease of doing business are just as important as ethical technology, sustainable design, and customer happiness. Not to mention accessibility, transparency, and inclusion.

Generational empowerment is also a critical element of this mission and mindset. Technology that fails along any of these lines is probably not something I want to build, or in which I want to invest. On the other hand, technology and innovation that increases and improves upward mobility, discovery, and humanity, is what Zen Ventures is all about. At a time when Instagram and GMail accounts can go missing out of the blue and customer service is non-existent, Zen Ventures exists to develop and promote technology that serves the interests and needs of both the people and the youth (more on this in Chapters 8 and 9). It all starts with the right mindset. It all starts with Zen.

5

The Six Myths
(1 & 2)

If nothing within you stays rigid, outward things will disclose themselves. Moving, be like water. Still, be like a mirror. Respond like an echo.

- Bruce Lee, *Tao of Jeet Kune Do*

Raising capital can be a bit of a black box. There are no standards or rational set of expectations on which one can depend. Founders often find themselves at the mercy of greedy Venture Capitalists. Human errors and insecurities exist everywhere you look.

On top of this, there are multiple investment myths that exist when it comes to Venture Capital, which is surprising for an industry that prides itself on due-diligence and verifiable results. Most of these myths are based on antiquated thinking and inherent cognitive bias, not to mention racial, gender, and age bias. The worst part about it, besides not being able to raise capital, is that Silicon Valley is one big echo chamber. People only receive information or opinions that reflect and reinforce their own. So the majority of these myths are believed and practiced by well over 90 percent of the funds and people in the industry. It's a kind of egotism and megalomania that you'll only fully appreciate when you visit Silicon Valley. You're likely to only find one decent human being out of one hundred.

This is somewhat predictable given the level of economic stratification in America, but it is, nonetheless, alarming. This level of group-think would be appalling for any industry in the world. The number of these myths is probably too high to count, but I've tried to list six of the most egregious and upsetting ones here. The list is by no means exhaustive, but should work to jumpstart a dialogue and debate about the proper course of action to take going forward.

Myth 1:

Startups Require Multiple Founders

(An Ode To Solopreneurs)

Oprah Winfrey, Sara Blakely, Magic Johnson, Mark Anastasi, Nate Weiner (Pocket). This is just a small list, a smattering if you will, of successful and notable Solopreneurs. By some estimates, there are over 41 million Solopreneurs in the world and they contribute over 1.3 trillion dollars to the United States economy. Yet according to the world of Venture Capital, Solopreneurship is dead and to be frowned upon. Startups, they argue, require multiple founders to be successful. This myth clearly falls into the category of things that VCs say or repeat that are blatantly false or incorrect. The problem is that it's simply not true. Although many VCs may believe or feel that startups with multiple founders do better or last longer, the real purpose of this myth is to block and limit the number of people who can receive capital. Like many of the other myths on the list, it's a way of propagating the status quo. Startups with multiple founders might very well do better than most Solopreneurs, but this is not an excuse to block Solopreneurs altogether. Yet this is exactly what we see happening in Silicon Valley and across the globe.

The truth is, like long-distance runners or lone sprinters, some people prefer, or are better off, working alone. It has nothing to do with being a "team player" or not. Some sports are played on teams others aren't. Can there be value in having multiple founders? Sure. I can't tell you how many times I've wished for an Eduardo Saverin type to save me from the cost of early startup fees; or a Jared Dunn type to take that business plan or prospectus off my hands. But the reality is, I work better alone. I shouldn't be forced to find a Cofounder at the last minute just to receive funding. Investors who require multiple founders are not only short-sighted but damaging and disruptive to the entrepreneurial process. Pass.

Myth 2:

You're Too Early.

Not Enough Traction or Revenue

Remember that scene from the movie *Forrest Gump* where Forrest can't find a seat on the bus? Then suddenly he finds an open seat, but one of the kids goes, "Seats Taken!" That's what it's like to hear the excuse "you're too early, not enough traction or revenue." Again, the true objective of this myth is to discriminate, block, or prohibit someone's "seat." It works to exclude and reduce the number of founders that get funded, and to clear the way for other, more established companies to thrive. But this policy, espoused as "State Doctrine," defeats the entire purpose of Venture Capital and Entrepreneurship; not to mention, it's usually applied arbitrarily and inconsistently.

I'm always confused by those VCs (even those run by friends of mine) that only invest in startups with millions of dollars in revenue or MRR. As a startup, that would defeat the entire purpose of raising capital, even if just for growth or expansion. VC debt capital is expensive and hard to come by. Why waste time and money raising capital when you have that much money in revenue already? Unless, of course, you're financing an acquisition or an IPO. But even then, there's probably cheaper capital out there. By that same logic, the notion that a startup needs revenue or overwhelming traction to be successful, especially at the seed or growth stage, is demonstrably untrue and counter to what bootstrapping is all about. A startup is not a small business. If you're looking to invest in a small business then you should probably be in Private Equity, not Venture Capital. That's a critical distinction. They don't call it *Venture* Capital for nothing.

The definition of the word "venture" is "a risky or daring journey or undertaking." To venture is to "dare to do something or go somewhere that may be dangerous or unpleasant." It's right there in the title. To deny a venture stage startup funding because they lack a certain level of traction or revenue is obviously an absurd notion. Of course, it's great to have revenue and traction as a startup, and as an investor I'd be happy to see it. But it shouldn't be a requirement or policy. I'm not investing in traction or revenue, I'm investing in a startup, a business idea, and a founder. Requiring revenue would be like requiring the elected President to be the "best" candidate. How do you define that? Rarely is that the case, and causation is not correlation.

Moreover, lack of traction or revenue is certainly not an invalidation of an idea, a startup, or a founder. In fact, I often find the highest returns hiding in the startups that are fresh from the farm with little to show but some milk and honey. They're less likely to have been picked at by the rabbits and competitors, and more likely to retain their secret sauce and trade secrets. They're just ripe. The idea that these fresh fruits are too early: Pass.

6

THE SIX MYTHS
(3 & 4)

Change before you have to.

- Jack Welch

Myth 3

A Pitch Has To Be Perfect & We Invest In People Not Ideas

Pitch contests have a unique way of devolving into the absurd. And perhaps the biggest flat out lie VCs tell themselves (but probably really believe) is that they invest in people not ideas. Allow me to explain why these two myths are not only deceptive and untrue, but philosophically problematic and psychologically unsettling. Given that 99 percent of venture capital goes to White male founders, when a VC says that they "invest in people not ideas," what they're really saying is that they invest in people that look and sound like them. Not you or me. It's a hidden cognitive bias, you see, but it speaks volumes about the industry.

The entire VC lexicon, "VC speak," can be unpacked and decrypted this way. Behind everything a VC says is a well-worn cognitive bias that betrays their true meaning and intent. Ideas are the lifeblood of the Startup Ecosystem. Without them we'd just be a bunch of incorporated logos and brands without any substance or significance. There'd be no there there. When a VC says they don't invest in ideas, what they're really doing is subtly criticizing you for not being far enough along yet for them to plunder your value. They're also creating a wall between themselves and all the half-baked ideas in the world that they would have to listen to if they didn't say such rubbish. VCs hear millions of pitches everyday. I suppose you can't blame them for trying to limit wasted time. But if we can't criticize them for half-truths, then they can't criticize us for calling them on their bullshit.

By that same logic, the idea that a pitch has to be perfect is flawed logic and a waste of everyone's time. The fact is that some founders just aren't good presenters or public speakers, and others would rather have their nails violently removed than parade themselves in front of a bunch of uptight assholes in a public pissing match, which they're more than likely bound to lose. I once attended a series of pitch contests in Silicon Valley that left me feeling sick to my stomach and without any faith left in humanity. I was in the middle of a raise and thought it'd be a fun experiment. Not so much. During one of the pitches a young female founder was publicly ridiculed and lambasted for being divorced. They humiliated her in front of everybody. I couldn't watch it was so bad. Nor could I understand why it was happening, but the judges seemed happy enough to go along with it. It was as though they were competing to see who could be the most ridiculous and obnoxious panelist. Afterward I was tempted to go up to the founder and give her the name of a good attorney so she could sue the pitch organizers for slander and intentional interference with economic gain. Cause that's exactly what it was.

The same thing happened to me at the next pitch when a grumpy old White guy decided to question and attack my numbers and traction. He couldn't believe how successful our MVP had been and made sure to let everyone know it. He even cursed at me and stuff. It was hilarious. I just laughed and smiled. Our numbers were rock solid. I think he was going through a divorce or something. Afterwards, someone did come up to me and suggest I sue him for discrimination and intentional infliction of emotional distress, not to mention slander. I might still do that.

What I discovered is that pitch contests are where disgruntled old lunatics go to feel important again. On the same day as the grumpy nay-sayer, one of the judges demanded that the participants do their pitches without looking at the screen. If anyone looked at the screen they were immediately disqualified. Like I said, lunatics! I'm all for memorizing your speeches and presentations, but if you can't look at the screen how would you know where you are? It's a ridiculous requirement to make any time, especially at the last minute. It goes to show that pitch contests and organizers miss the entire point. They're so busy focusing on the dynamics of the presentation that they completely miss the big idea, and the big picture. A pitch is not an exercise in public speaking or rhetoric. Judges are supposed to be listening to the strength and validity of the idea, not judging founders for their oratory, speaking skills, or appearance; and certainly not their love lives. This seems obvious to me and many others, but the majority of pitch contests out there are still absolute nightmares.

Pitching VCs directly, although not as humiliating, tends to be the same way. I've done hundreds or VC pitches now and can honestly report that, by and large, they completely miss the point of the conversation, ask outdated and *accusatory* questions, and bury themselves behind so many cognitive biases that I can barely keep count. Again, this practice is intentional and meant to limit, scare, disrupt, block, and abuse founders from moving forward. What kind of industry eats and destroys its own investments before they're even up and running? The entire VC process is counterintuitive to good entrepreneurship, innovation, and economics. In this way, VCs have become their own worst enemy. Unfortunately, we're the ones who suffer, especially diverse founders. Pass.

Myth 4:

Raising Capital Should Be Stressful

Raising capital doesn't have to be stressful. If anyone tells you otherwise, they're your enemy. Making founders miserable seems to be the hidden objective of most VCs. What does that tell you? I think Silicon Valley gets it from Wall Street, where young Goldman Sachs Associates are treated like trash and hazed endlessly until they quit or cry. If I had a dollar for every young investment banker or trainee I've seen cry because their job is so stressful I'd be a billionaire. Somewhere deep down inside, seasoned investment bankers and VCs want to pass this pain and suffering along to others. If they had to go through it, so do you! There's also the element of wanting to steal the energy, thunder, and ideas of the entrepreneurs. If the TV show *Silicon Valley* is any indication, most VCs were not very popular in high school and are now eager to be "the Belles of the Ball." Sometimes they see their young counterparts as the competition instead of as colleagues. Most first-time founders are probably too naive to know the difference.

The question remains: Why would you want to damage and undercut someone you're about to invest in, or in whom you might invest someday? The myth that startups have to be stressful is completely erroneous. It's the perfect example of the flawed thinking of the industry. Raising money for your startup does not have to be a stressful or negative experience. In fact, it should be quite fun and invigorating. That's what Zen Ventures is all about. Founders should be catapulted forward with all the resources they need to be successful, not dragged down by silly people, immature emotions, and red tape. Every competitive economy in the world knows this, except, it seems, the United States. Why? Perhaps because here we're more concerned with protecting the boys club and blocking access to capital than supporting diversity, equity, and inclusion. Unfortunately, we see the investment process as a process of elimination and a way of perpetuating the status quo, rather than as a mature process meant to support young Entrepreneurs and foster innovation. Pass.

7

THE SIX MYTHS
(5 & 6)

Awareness is the greatest agent for change.

- Zen Proverb

Myth 5:

Diverse Founders Are High Risk

The number one myth in Venture Capital is that diverse founders are a risky investment. The fallout from this fallacy can be seen throughout the country. It's reflected in our income disparities, gender imbalances, and racial and economic inequalities, which are alarmingly persistent in our country. The benefit of being a Civil Rights Leader, a Founder, and a Venture Capitalist is that I get to see the industry from all sides. And I must say that despite all the recent fanfare and whitewashing around diversity in the industry, the outlook for diverse founders is still incredibly bad. Studies show that diversity greatly improves profitability, but attitudes surrounding diverse Founders, especially Black founders, remain ambiguous and antagonistic. There's still the micro-aggressive mentality that one must first prove themselves capable as a person first, a founder second, and then prove their readiness and viability for investment third. We're made to jump through multiple hurdles and hoops while our White counterparts go straight through. This is not just an unnecessary process, it's a painful one. One that continuously reminds diverse founders of their supposed inferiority and obvious inequality. Imagine if that were you or your kids having to endure the burden of being second class citizens in both the social realm and the business realm on a daily basis.

These stigmas and stereotypes have real world consequences for our economy and our society. New studies show that the cost of inequality and discrimination in venture capital exceeds 11 trillion dollars! This is not an arbitrary or insignifiant number. It's a number that has the potential to sink the entire global economy. This is not political speculation or ideological banter, it's a matter of Economic fact. That's why President Biden and Vice President Harris have prioritized anti-discrimination and Economic

Empowerment initiatives in their first 100 days in office.

I've written extensively about technological and algorithmic inequality, but it bears repeating here. The kind of discrimination and inequality we're dealing with out in Silicon Valley and across the country is embedded into the very frameworks, processes, and platforms we use to make decisions about everything from funding and credit to housing and education, wages, employment, dating, health, policy, and, of course, policing. How is it that the very systems our country has come to rely on are often knowingly, purposefully, and inherently biased, discriminatory, and backwards? Now you know. For example, studies show that the Risk Beta for diverse founders is, in fact, better than that of their White counterparts. Additionally we still use telephone numbers and cell phone data to make decisions about creditworthiness. These data are used to make decisions about who should or should not receive a loan or mortgage despite evidence of massive irregularities in these data, and the very high potential for identity theft and fraud. Creditors assess everything, from what websites you visit to how charged you keep your phone, in making decisions about your credit. This is absurd and highly susceptible to discmination and abuse. Pass!

Myth 6:

All About The Technicals

Myth number 6 is a catch all for the myriad of technical myths that exist in the industry and are actively propounded by VCs, big and small. It includes things like: Technical Founders are better than Non-Technical Founders, Sweat Equity doesn't count, and a whole list of other technical requirements VCs place on startups and founders before they're even fully up and running. I'm sure you've heard a few. The American economy should exist to support startups and small businesses. It's an economic imperative. As we've seen, in the age of globalization, the more roadblocks you create for businesses the more likely they are to take their business elsewhere: China, India, Dubai, Europe, you name it. There's nothing stopping startups from taking their companies elsewhere. Yet the industry still operates to limit funding and support rather than expand, widen, and increase it. None of the mythical technical requirements VCs place on startups have any actual bearing or authority over founders or their businesses. Yet for some reason they've become a part of the lexicon. I really couldn't tell you how such shortsightedness ever came to exist. My guess is that a few experienced investors had favorable outcomes from these myths and lobbied the industry to make them permanent. Like whether a startup is incorporated as a C Corporation or an S Corporation in Delaware or their home state, these myths are by and large a matter of preference. Yet they're espoused as gospel to the people. This is a profoundly dangerous and deceptive cycle. Laws and regulations governing Accreditation, Taxes, Data Privacy, and Insurance are one thing. But myths, preferences, and falsehoods meant to discriminate, undermine, and exclude are another. Pass.

8

OUR VISION & MODEL

Good business leaders create a vision, articulate the vision, passionately own the vision, and relentlessly drive it to completion.

- Jack Welch

Mobility, Discovery, Humanity

The greatest gift we can give ourselves and each other is upward mobility. Life is not about attaining things, but discovering ourselves and the world around us. And without our humanity we would just be another species of animals. Mobility, discovery, humanity. These are the three pillars of Zen Ventures and the foundation of our vision, mission, and model. Think about the Universe, the stars, the galaxies, and everything still left to be explored and discovered. How will we get there? What will we find? And what will we bring with us? These are the questions we ask ourselves at Zen Ventures. You're headed to outer space and can only bring 5 things with you, what are they? Those are the areas in which we focus our technology, startups, and investments. Those 5 items are the future.

Hybrid technologies and products, Open Architectures, Automation, AI, Gaming, Big Data and FutureTech are also major parts of our investment model. They are the processes, methodologies, and approaches that will drive the future forward. At Zen Ventures, we envision a time when startups and investing will be almost completely automated. Our proprietary investment platform, Daedalus, integrates the best in automated design, analytics, computer vision, research, and social listening with next generation automatic machine learning (AutoML) and artificial intelligence to create a seamless 360 degree investment and development process. Daedalus can run on its own and will eventually include things like automated patents, portfolios, and valuations. From start to finish, the capabilities include advanced search, engineering, investment, and design. As soon as Daedalus discovers a good idea or untapped opportunity it goes to work researching the market, identifying key trends, and preparing our portfolio for a new position or product down to the algorithm.

Kinetic, human-centered design goes hand-in-hand with our investment model: Clean, simple, minimal, extensible, usable, flexible, and interoperable. These are the design principles by which we live and swear. Our product development process is a unique one. We call it Quad-Quad Waterfall. It is a streamlined evolution of the Agile and Waterfall development methodologies and brings together the best of both worlds through rapid prototyping, overlapping programming timelines, and simultaneous development. Together, these methods, techniques, and processes have yielded some significant breakthroughs, patents, trade secrets, and startups, including: Pommel and AdHeat (FinTech and AdTech); Lavalytics and Drip Data (Big Data Transformation and Decision Intelligence); Fluid and Dreidl (Quantum Computing, CleanTech and FutureTech); GroupIQ, Quail, LizAI, MagicAI, and Mordecai (Advanced AI Platforms, Cyber Security, and Conversational Intelligence); RegenRx, PulseID, and OpenRx

(BioTech, Pharma, and Health & Wellness); VYNL (Verified AI Robustness Algorithm); Quwench (In-game Hydration and Precision Dosing Products); Basta Pasta (Fruit & Banana-based Pasta Sauces); Emerald Water and Wasabi Water (CBD, plant, and nut-infused water brands); and a long list of other innovations and breakthroughs, including, DropTech, AdaptTech, FastTech, Disposables, and a new proposed Proof for the Navier-Stokes Equation, one of the ten remaining problems in Mathematics and Physics, as identified by the Millennium Prize.

Then there's our focus on Social Impact. When it comes to Impact, there are world-changing ideas hiding behind every corner, under every rock, and in every water stream. The ways of the world may change, but the opportunity for breakthrough and impact remains. Technology, Entertainment, and Design (TED) is all about finding the best ideas worth sharing. Science, Technology, Engineering, and Math (STEM) and Science, Technology, Engineering, Art, and Maths (STEAM) is about preparing students for the future. The Millennium Development Goals (MDGs), Sustainable Development Goals (SDGs) and The Millennium Prize in Mathematics exist for a reason: To improve the world, impact the future, and set us on a more sustainable course. These impact programs (and many others) are more than just acronyms; they serve as the bedrock and wellspring of social, economic, and scientific evolution and opportunity in the world, not just fancy nomenclature. This is what Zen Ventures is all about. These platforms are deeply integrated into our core business model, mission, vision, and philosophy.

As a young Digital Strategist at the World Bank, I helped design and develop some of the earliest frameworks for Open Data and the use of Information and Communication Technology for Development (ICT4D). In other words, Digital Transformation, Systems Change, and Global Development. At the heart of this process is a heavy focus on innovation, modernization, and core systems integration. What we learned and shared with the world are the best ways in which platforms and services can be used to diminish conflict, improve human services and progress, and connect economies. Interestingly, the process had more to do with removing biases and roadblocks than adding new gimmicks and gadgets. More importantly, we did this while protecting privacy and identity, and empowering women and children. It taught us about the *real* cost of capital for both the developed and the developing world, a problem that continues to plague global founders, VCs, and startups to this day. In mapping the structure and nature of global conflict for the 2011 World Development Report (WDR), we were able to design a new roadmap to help move the world in the right direction. A roadmap similar to the one we propose here.

Later on, as a Digital strategist at Havas, a global Creative Agency, I helped advise the team at the UN Foundation on the packaging, design, and delivery of the Millennium Development Goals (MDGs)—now the Sustainable Development Goals (SDGs)—the list of top social, economic, and environmental priorities to reach by 2025 - 2030. We must continue to prioritize these efforts and embed them ever more deeply into our global business and economic outlooks and efforts. This is why we've chosen to align our model with the SDGs and the Millennium Prize at Zen Ventures. These frameworks will continue well into the future and provide the foundation for future innovation. Zen Ventures will continue to push them forward.

9

OUR STARTUPS & PORTFOLIO

Zen vibes only.

- Zen Ventures

At Zen Ventures we design, develop, and build our startups internally. That is the essence of a boutique maker/builder startup studio. We also develop, package, and produce original content and intellectual property (IP). Our catalogue mixes gaming, film, TV, scripted and unscripted series, reality series, branded content, commercial production, publishing, fiction and nonfiction, children's books, and academic books. Our IP portfolio includes patents, trademarks, copyrights, databases, music catalogues, trade secrets, algorithms, and proprietary lists, techniques, processes, methods, and models. But our most important elements are creativity, play, authenticity, and originality.

We are founder friendly, category and platform agnostic, and forward thinking. We focus on "No Brainers," outstanding design, breakthrough discoveries, and advanced capabilities. We're for simplicity, minimalism, and craftsmanship. Elegance, aesthetics, and accessibility. We look for the designers, developers, and dramatists of the future to help bring our startups and projects to life. We embrace equity-based compensation and super casual work environments. We support the artists and dreamers among us. And most importantly, we keep things Zen. Our current categories include:

- Leisure & Events
- AI & Automation
- Food & Beverage
- Patents & IP
- FinTech & PropTech
- BioTech, AgTech & Pharma
- Analytics, Big Data & BI
- Music, Gaming, Media & Entertainment
- FutureTech & DeepTech
- E-commerce & Other

Leisure & Events

ZenFest, ZenLeague & ZenCamp

The flagship startups of the Zen Ventures portfolio

are our branded online and offline events and leisure series, including: ZenFest, ZenLeague, and ZenCamp. ZenFest is our super chill music and technology festival. ZenLeague is our Fantasy Startup League. And ZenCamp is our future-focused casual youth coding camp. Investing should be fun and perhaps somewhat competitive. That's the idea behind ZenLeague. Like Fantasy Football, it's a great way for you and your friends to test each other's prowess and performance when it comes to investing. Grab a group of friends and select your favorite founders and startups. Measure their progress over time and see who performs the best. The league with the highest ROI wins and gets rewarded. Simple, fun and entertaining. Not to mention a great way to build and optimize your portfolio.

Coding is a critical skill, but programming has evolved. Low code and No code will continue to grow and impact the industry. So will coding automation and automated Machine Learning (AutoML). With ZenCamp, we plan to promote and prepare the next generation of coders and coding languages. We've developed some of our own languages, like Dreidl, and are designing cutting edge products and platforms using underrepresented languages like Python, R, and Wolfram (Mathematica). We believe ZenCamp will produce the very best of the next generation of coders and coding innovations. ZenFest speaks for itself. After all that coding and investing, our fans will need somewhere to go to relax, enjoy their favorite artists and music (including those from our own roster), and unwind. Together, ZenFest, ZenLeague, and ZenCamp make the perfect trio of events and activities. Waitlists are already available online. We hope you'll join us.

AI & Automation

AI and Automation are not only the future of technology, but the future of Social Impact, as well. That's why it's the largest part of our portfolio. Temporal Automation, Conversational Servers and AI, In-Memory Computing, and Converged AI. We know that in the future your brain will automate and optimize your experience, servers will talk to each other verbally (they already do in many ways), and AI will deliver its value verbally, visually and in real-time. Zen Ventures is already there. Our customers say "LizAI, optimize my website," and she does it perfectly. They say "Ludwig, optimize logistics," and he does it. I say "SleepAI, improve my sleep. DreamcatcherAI, record my dream, and Mordecai, optimize my day," and they do it. I say "HealthAI, improve my memory and nutrition," and I immediately feel better. I say "InvestAI, optimize my portfolio," and it does it. Welcome to the future!

Our AI and Automation technology spans several categories and focus areas, including: Personal Assistants & Productivity, Team and Business Intelligence, Logistics, Mobile and Cross-platform Apps, the Future of Work, Health & Wellness, Data & Analytics, Government & Civic Technology, Money & Investing, Research, Cyber Security, Military Technology, and BioInformatics:

Personal Assistants & Productivity

- LizAI
- Mordecai
- Estately
- Firmly
- Concierge

- Pushkin

Automation & Analysis

- GroupIQ
- Talos
- Skematic
- Kaleidoscope
- Relay

Real-Time Analysis & Action

- Snapcount
- Solve
- Vectr
- Sensei
- Timbr
- SentimentAI

Ambient & Advanced AI

- DreamcatcherAI
- MagicAI
- SleepAI
- SenseAI

GovTech & CivicTech (Suite/Platform)

- DiplomacyAI
- PolicyAI
- DemocracyAI
- GovAI
- ConstitutionAI
- MilitaryAI
- PoliceAI
- HealthAI
- LawAI
- PatentAI

Health & Wellness

- NutritionAI
- FortifyAI
- MetaMind (Neurolinguistics & Brain Training)

Research & Education

- InterpretAI
- TutorAI
- EducateAI
- SearchAI
- ResearchAI
- ReferenceAI

Media, Marketing & Design

- AdsAI
- ColorAI
- UXAI

Cyber Security

- Quail
- CyberAI
- ProtectionAI
- GENGHIS

Money

- CreditAI
- MoneyAI
- TaxesAI
- InsuranceAI
- InvestAI

Logistics & Infrastructure

- DeliveryAI
- ConstructionAI
- Ludwig

Algorithms & AutoML

- HorusAI
- SlinkyAI
- CortexAI
- UnanimousAI
- Aspen Trees

Food & Beverage

Food & Beverage is a 12 trillion dollar industry, perhaps the biggest out there. It is a global market with implications for Agriculture, Health & Wellness, Food Security, and many more critical human-centered concerns. It is also one of the best markets for memorable and meaningful brands. Traditionally, Food & Beverage has been dominated by a small group of conglomerates, but this is quickly changing. Small players and innovative shops like Innoviom and Vertosa are making big moves and starting to command large portions of the market. Mergers and acquisitions with the major players are on the rise owing to major capitalization and expansion opportunities. In steps Zen Ventures with a focus on hybrids, infusions, nanotechnology, advanced nutrition, hydration and endurance, digestion, pet care, waste reduction and micro-packaging, personalization and 3D Printing, food combinatorics, the future of gastronomy, and flavor.

From Banana Flavored Pasta Sauce (Basta Pasta) to BrewBrew (Nano Beer) and Psychedelic Soba (Mushroom Noodles), our Food & Beverage brands are bold, brilliant, and delicious. We're pushing the envelope on what's possible in the culinary arts and gastronomy. We're also focused on the future of consumption, hydration, and micro-dosing. Quwench, our In-Game Hydration and Micro-Dosing Technology company sits at the center of several trillion-dollar industries, including: Sports & Fitness, Food & Beverage, Nutrition & Wellness, Pharma & Medical, and Cannabis. Our growing list of Food & Beverage brands includes:

- Basta Pasta (Fruit-Flavored Pasta Sauce)
- Cannolis (Flavored Edibles & Rolling Papers)
- Gyunyu (CBD-infused Milks)
- Ceviche-to-Go
- BrewBrew (Traditional Zulu Nano Beer)
- Lava Pizza (Hawaiian Lava Pizza)

ZEN VENTURES

- Yum Yum Layercakes (Fried Noodle Patties)
- Yankee Fish & Chips
- Wasabi Water
- PB Water
- Water Nut
- Agua De Dios
- Bill's Beer Chips (Beer Potato Chips)
- Potion (Cannabis Tea & Coffee)
- Oatmeal Water
- Emerald Water
- Lily's Lau Lau (Hawaiian Lau Lau)
- Stromboli Slut
- Laika (Pet Care & CBD products)
- Psychedelic Soba (Mushroom Noodles)
- CannaCart (Cannabis Food Truck)

Patents & IP

Patents and Intellectual Property (IP) are the bread and butter of our venture studio. The portfolio spans several industries and focus areas. It consists of utility, design, and plant patents, including:

- Blockchain Encryption Technology
- Advanced Research Platforms
- The XR Headset (VR/AR)
- Geospatial Analytics Platforms
- The Hourglass Wine Decanter
- The Flightpack
- The Banana Pistol
- The Stable State Spacecraft
- The Diamond ETL Schema
- The Organic Seasoning Branch
- The Fluid Liquid Quantum Computer
- Smart Karate Gis and Yoga Mats

ZEN VENTURES

- The Coffee Bean Steering Wheel
- VYNL Advanced AI Robustness Technique
- The Edible Wine Bottle
- The Quwench Liquid-release Mouthguard
- Dating Apps
- Advanced Algorithms
- FutureTech Fashion & Luggage
- Triangular Banking Tech (The Tokyo Move)

FinTech & PropTech

Pommel & Bequeath

~

Pommel

Bank, buy and invest with IP Assets

An asset properly defined is not an arbitrary thing. For far too long, however, the assets and markets we rely upon in our economy have been defined arbitrarily.

The same can be said about credit ratings and risk profiles. Risk-averse investors often overlook perfectly viable opportunities due to bad credit data and cognitive bias when, in fact, a risk-neutral approach would better serve their interests. This often leads to imbalances in the marketplace from which the economy often struggles to recover. That's exactly what's happening in Silicon Valley at the moment as VCs continue to pay lip service to black founders without actually transferring funds. It really is their loss.

We often forget that fiat money is a government-issued currency that is not backed by a physical commodity, such as gold or silver, but rather by the government that issues it. Assets such as Patents, Trademarks, Copyrights, Databases, Music Royalties, and even Trade Secrets (IP Assets) would make far more reliable and tangible sources of value and income.

That's where the majority of the market value is anyway. For example, a 2017 study found that intangible assets accounted for 84 percent of the S&P 500's total market value, whereas tangible assets were only 16 percent. The same was true for the CSI 300 Index. Indeed, intangible assets are responsible for 84 percent of all business value. Hence the old saying, wealth is in the mind. Yet there's still no easy way for everyday consumers to take advantage of the inherent value of their IP Assets. Until now.

Enter Pommel, a new platform for monetizing IP Assets. Pommel is a platform and marketplace for converting intellectual property assets into tangible capital assets. Our goal is to make it easier to buy and sell goods and services by determining the true market value of intellectual property, thereby creating a virtuous cycle between IP owners and merchants. Our hope is that someday soon, everyone will be able to do things like make purchases, buy real estate, improve their credit, and pay tuition with their IP Assets alone. We believe this is the future of finance.

BioTech, AgTech & Pharma

RegenRx, OpenRx, Top Soil & Pulse ID

Neuro and Biotechnology are the most interesting and complex emerging fields, with Agricultural Technology and Pharmaceuticals not far behind. Given their relative size of investment in Research and Development (R&D), the biggest breakthroughs in the industry will most likely occur across these fast-moving sectors. Zen Ventures will be there, too. Our growing group of brands includes:

- RegenRx (Regenerative Pharma & Technology)

- OpenRx (Open-source Drug R&D)
- Top Soil (Mobile AgTech & Crop Intelligence)
- PulseID (BioInformatics and IoT Health)

In the years ahead, we plan to expand into Advanced Nanotechnology and Neuroscience, including human-to-computer interfaces, in-memory computing, advanced drug delivery, and Adaptive Technology. There is a huge opportunity to improve business ethics and integrity in this space. New legislation will begin to emerge along these lines.

Analytics, Big Data & BI

Lavalytics, Recap & Drip Data

~

Lavalytics

Enterprise Decision Intelligence

Information Analytics is a 1 trillion dollar industry. Decision Intelligence is the cutting edge. Lavalytics is the tip of the spear. The platform sits at the center of the data stack and integrates the most unique set of third-party plugins on the market. It's the crystal ball for your business and the Dyson of Data Analytics. Our advanced NLP and patented Diamond ETL Schema makes Predictive Analytics easy and accessible. Our new Verified AI Robustness Algorithm, VYNL adds an additional layer of security, especially for AI Clients, including: Autonomous Vehicles, Programmatic Advertising, Facial Recognition, R&D, Computer Vision, Conversational AI, and Cyber Security. Our ability to gain insights from big data has failed to keep pace with the amount of data available. Over 73 percent of big data projects are not profitable. We want to make it easier and more accessible to go from query to solution, increasing speed to insight and revenue for your business, university, or non-profit. By making your data more useful, we make the world's data more relevant and valuable. Our full set of features will include:

- Augmented Analytics & Spatial ETL
- Unstructured Data Integration & Visualization
- 3D Business Intelligence Mapping
- Competitive Global Intelligence
- Analytics As A Service (AaaS)
- Deep AutoML
- No coding or SQL required

- Endless scalability and integrations
- Rapid Intelligence Analysis & Visualization
- Whitelabel access and cross-platform portability
- Open Source API and Developer Network

Our target industries include:

- Music, Media & Entertainment
- Advertising & Marketing
- Aerospace & Engineering
- Consumer Products
- Sports & Fashion
- Gaming & Social
- Telecoms & IT
- Finance & Banking
- Retail & Real Estate
- Human Capital & Recruitment

- Energy, Automotive & IoT
- Education & Non-Profits
- Pharma & Healthcare
- Research & Emerging Markets
- Mining & Construction
- Government & Civil Service

As businesses continue to become more automated and informed, Lavalytics will become a leading player in this space.

Music, Gaming, Media & Entertainment

Music, Gaming, Media and Entertainment is the most promising and exciting category in our portfolio. Zen Ventures develops, packages, and will eventually produce original content across gaming, film, TV, scripted and unscripted series, reality series, branded content, commercial production, publishing, fiction and nonfiction, children's books, and academic books. With over 500 projects in development, our content is all about originality, creativity, and authenticity. Our technology and projects include:

- YogaMates (A Dating App for Yogis)
- AdHeat (AdTech)
- Test Pilot (AI for Film/TV Development)
- Gi Ninja (Interactive Sports Fitness)
- Showrunnr (TV Showrunning Technology)
- Libro (Instant Publishing)
- Splendid (Advanced Content Curation)
- Splattr (Paintballing & Content)
- Death Ray (Global Production Company)
- Grapevine (Mobile Streaming App)
- JYNGL (Real-time Ads & Ringtones)

- Blogger Underground (Investigative Journalism)
- My Rider (Smart Music Riders)
- Yul-Bow & Young Xi (Chinese Hip-Hop Duo)
- The Heavy Hitters (Rap MCs)
- The Night Snipers (Electronic & EDM band)
- The Clap von Clap Offs (Indie Synth-Pop Band)

FutureTech & DeepTech

FutureTech and DeepTech were some of the first categories added to Zen Ventures given our focus on mobility, evolution, and the future. We are on the front lines of scientific breakthrough and innovation. Several of our startups cross FutureTech, DeepTech and SpaceTech. Others focus on Advanced Quantum Computing, Transportation, Hardware, Networks, and the Internet of Things (IoT). Our current list of startups in this space includes:

- Bounce (Pogo-Transportation)
- Dreidl (Next Generation Hydroelectricity)
- Fluid (Liquid Vanadium Quantum Computers)
- Incredible WiFi (OTT WiFi)

E-commerce & Other

E-commerce is quickly becoming the most important sector in the industry. It has been a staple of our portfolio for some time now. In addition to these brands, there are a number of startups in the portfolio that don't fit neatly into any one category. In the coming months, we'll also be launching additional funds connected to Zen Ventures, including Just Ventures, The Family Fund, and Bookmark Capital. The complete list in this category includes:

- Manboo Bamboo (Authentic Bamboo Products)
- Gazebo (Automated Delivery)
- Prayer Party (Spiritual Nonprofit)
- Veterans United (Veterans Nonprofit)
- Just Ventures (Law & Society Fund)
- Bookmark Capital (Capital for Writers)
- The Family Fund (Family-Friendly Capital)
- Virtuous Cycles (Spinning & Touring Bikes)
- Champ's Condoms (Reproductive Health)

10

THE FUTURE OF VENTURE CAPITAL & IMPACT INVESTING

The future of Venture Capital is automated investing and working from the beach without a single worry in mind.

- Zen Ventures

Now that we've taken a walk through the mythical forest of Silicon Valley, let us embark on a more solid and fruitful roadmap towards the future of Venture Capital and Impact Investing. Close your eyes and imagine the most ideal version of the startup landscape and fundraising process. This is where our new journey begins and the old one ends. Now let's play start, stop, repeat. What should be improved about the process? What should be eliminated or corrected? And what should be extended or enlarged based on our new outlook and direction?

Entrepreneurship, ideas, innovation, and intellectual property are the lifeblood of our economy; they should be protected, supported, and celebrated at all costs. Piracy, corporate crime and espionage must be vigorously challenged, countered, and eliminated. Simplicity, accessibility, usability, and ease of doing business must take precedence. Consumer protection and customer service must become corporate priorities again. And the power dynamic between founders and VCs, startups and conglomerates, bootstrappers and mega-billionaires must become more balanced. We should champion Solopreneurship, nascent ideas, and non-technical founders as much as everything else. We should promote diversity, equity, and inclusion in real, actionable, and tangible ways, not slick PR campaigns, whitewashing, and lip service everytime another black man is killed in America.

We can dispel the idea that raising capital has to be stressful, overwhelming, and unfair. And we can push back collectively and constructively against the myths and absurd preferences of an elite few. That's just for starters. Eventually we can and must find ways to eliminate preferential treatment and bias altogether, and begin to automate some of the more inclusive and equitable practices we've discussed. We can improve our infrastructure, networks, and pipelines so that they're more inclusive, responsive, and accessible to the people. In so doing, we can make our economy more resilient and globally competitive while improving local outcomes, as well.

Given the rapid rate of technological change and innovation, this is an exercise that should be improved upon and repeated every year or two, if not every quarter. This way we can begin to better track our progress and measure our performance along key indicators. And we can do all this while respecting the rule of law, operating ethically and sustainably, and adhering to the collective values and cultures of all countries, not just our own. The people are ready for improvements and reforms along these lines, and the future demands it.

On a higher, more spiritual, level we can begin to incorporate the lessons and values of Zen Buddhism into our lives and businesses in a way that bolsters productivity, happiness, and customer and employee satisfaction. We can leverage the Eightfold Path, wonderful moments, and Ubuntu to improve customer service, product satisfaction, and design. We can take the Right View when it comes to revenue, social impact, and economic opportunity. We can let our Social Entrepreneurs lead from the front, not from behind, by designing and scaling businesses, bottom lines, and beneficial commercial practices that improve overall security, sustainability, and well-being. And we can put young people (Millennials and Gen-Z) in the driver's seat when it comes to strategy, policy, and commerce. In case you didn't realize, we're not asking we're demanding it.

So what does the future hold for Venture Capital and Impact Investing. There's no doubt that Automation, Artificial Intelligence, and Gaming will continue to have a tremendous impact on the industry and the economy. The same is true for Neuro-Technology, BioTech, and FutureTech, including Quantum Computing and SpaceTech. One could speculate about the exact manner in which these technologies will come together and impact the future, but the purpose would be lost on an industry that is not yet ready to embrace these innovations, identify the best ideas, and adopt the proper mindset about their proper implementation.

Essence precedes existence, and time is of the essence. We must adopt the right mindset about the future before we can bring it about in its greatest form. Too few people are reaping the benefits and rewards of a broken system. Too few people are benefiting at the expense of others. This is the way of upheaval and strife, not progress and perfection. We must observe and question the very performance of the industry before we can move forward; VCs should take caution when it comes to deciding on the biggest issues and ideas to tackle first.

There must be major reforms and innovations in Banking, Credit and Capital Markets, Insurance, Lending, Real Estate, and Consumer Protection before we can move forward properly, especially for Millennials and Gen-Z. A psychological assessment of the VCs in charge of capital would be incredibly helpful, too. Who are these people in control of our economy? What are their true motivations and agendas? What do they think about the World, society, and their role in it? What are their true insecurities, biases, and beliefs? And how do those impact their decision making, outlook, and investments? They know so much about us, yet we still know so little about them. They hold an almost absolute power over our futures as founders and consumers, yet their power goes unchecked.

What do we know about the future? Well, for one thing, we know that the outlook will be bleak if VCs are allowed to continue operating the way they do. The invisible hand of the market is not so invisible to us after all. Thus, the market itself must be made ethical and true. Diversity, equity, and inclusion must be made real. And finally, those with a voice and the power to change things must step out of the shadows and into the light. Zen Ventures will continue to lead the way.

ABOUT THE AUTHOR

Champion Muthle aka Daniel Maree is an award-winning Writer-Director, Creative and Cultural Strategist, Independent Journalist, Publisher, Civil Rights Leader, Inventor, Philosopher, Creative Technologist, Afro-Futurist, and Social Entrepreneur. He is a Frederick Douglass Scholar and Forbes 30 Under 30 Honoree for Social Entrepreneurship. His work has been featured in the MoMA and the Library of Congress.

www.ingramcontent.com/pod-product-compliance
Lightning Source LLC
Chambersburg PA
CBHW020445220526
45464CB00002B/867